Where Rivers Run Deep

# Where Rivers Run Deep
Narratives: 1962-1972

by

Don Gutteridge

*First Edition*

This edition includes:
Part One of *Death at Quebec and Other Poems*
(Fiddlehead Books, 1971)

*Saying Grace: An Elegy*
(Fiddlehead Books, 1972)

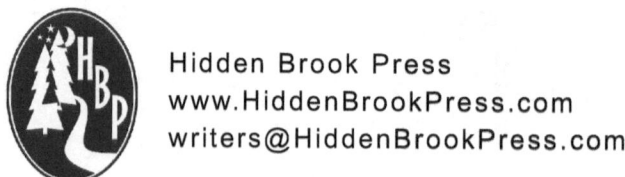

Hidden Brook Press
www.HiddenBrookPress.com
writers@HiddenBrookPress.com

Where Rivers Run Deep: Narratives: 1962-1972
by Don Gutteridge

Cover Design – Sol Terlson Kennedy
Layout and Design – Richard M. Grove

Typeset in Garamond
Printed and bound in Canada
Distributed in USA by Ingram,
          in Canada by Hidden Brook Distribution


Library and Archives Canada Cataloguing in Publication

Title: Where rivers run deep : narratives, 1962-1972 /
by Don Gutteridge.
Other titles: Poems. Selections (2021 : Hidden Brook Press)
Names: Gutteridge, Don, 1937- author.
Description: Narrative poems.
Identifiers: Canadiana (print) 2021020978X |
          Canadiana (ebook) 20210209852 |
          ISBN 9781989786390 (softcover) |
          ISBN 9781989786406 (ebook)
Classification: LCC PS8513.U85 A6 2021 |
          DDC C811/.54—dc23

# Table of Contents

# Epilogue
A Poem for Four Voices

## 1 The Jesuits in Huronia

Bringing our Word
we came
to what we thought
was wilderness

Knew
the hard spring
rivers rock
against the cross
of muscle   bone
down the spine
we kept
as secret joy
(remembered Calvaries)

Knew
a wind of ice
flung like shale
against the flesh
(St. Stephen upright
leaning into pain)
and winter then
providing snow
and wilderness enough
for forty Moses

Bringing our Light
we came
to what we thought
was Darkness,
and found

These faces
bright with summer
innocence and
knowing of winter
running cold
in primal stone

Bringing our Gift
we came
to what we thought
was Emptiness,
and found

a rib of life
more green
than Adam's
dream of Eden
lost

And found

another name
for love
a masculinity
of pine and seed
of suns unrepressed
beneath the
mothering earth awaits
lightning's release:
electric darkness

Bringing our Light   our Gift
we came
bringing our Word
to what we thought was dumbness

                                      of rock
                                      of pagan rib

and found

          a lightning shock
          to numb the soul
          dumbfounding flesh

Until we seemed
but only tongues
dropping syllables
into Chaos

and no reply
but
Babylon.

## 2  Champlain

When I left my name
in passing
on a river
on a lake
did it bleed
when spring came
to crack the ice
capillaries of
sudden freedom?
did it burn
with summer's
skin of sun and
water warm beneath?
did it die
with autumn and
slow funeral of leaves
moved thru river
before cold closed
on fall and all
there was of death?
till spring and
new transfusions
of sun
could make
another dying
for river
for lake
bearing my name.

But did the letters
bleed?
The syllables
burn?
My name admit to
death?

Or did it
(left in passing)
merely pass
the way
that all our names
must pass
when blood
is silent,
our bones mute?

And yet,
I *was* there:
on those rivers
that lake,
felt my
paddle-blade
touch a summer
running in the deep current
saw the
image of my death
in maples
exposed to sudden
wilderness of age,
measured the
quality of winter
ice corrosion
with a linkage
of my own.

Did I give
my name
(in passing)
to lake   to river?

Or did I give
my name up
to river and lake
in a passing
in a moving
beyond word
and name
            to a last
            syllable
            of blood?

## 3 Hudson

When I came
to this place
to this wide bay
I had seen men die:
husk of their bodies
curved over
worm of scurvy
feeding inside,
had seen the
simple bullet
find a core
of flesh,
or blade break
a stem of
arm or leg,
letting death
in
and the eyes
reluctant
feeling it.

When I came
with my ship
and my self
to this place
I had seen
many deaths.

But there is no
death like this:
with the whole
sea soured
with fish rotting
in ice
of elemental graves,

and wind blowing
conflagration
of cold over
pine and tamarack
that have been
burned beyond
burning and
still green
somewhere
at the charred
brains of
their growing
at roots of rock
with grain of
resurrection
still in them.

There is no death
like this one:
my blood souring
and the sea around me,
my mind burning
with a wind's flame,
my flesh rotting
in an elemental grave,
and somewhere
with eyes just
beginning
I reach thru
charred remains of
flesh   bone   brain
for root of
resurrection
I never knew
till now

till this burning
till this death
on a wide bay
in the private ark
I built
of my self,
though ice
closes
      elemental
        over
          me.

## 4  Riel

### 1

I am a man
as any man:

> hands to know
> the plough's hand
> deeper in the earth,
> hair to feel
> the wind's
> passing thru
> and grasses move,
> eyes to let
> the sky's
> vastness in
> to deeper skies
> I only know
> because
> my hands
> my hair
> these eyes
> become a voice
> to say

I am a man

## 2

There is no
eloquence to
blood running
from the mouths
of wounds and
battles lost,
the eyes of the dead
at Duck Lake
and Batoche are
white stones
darkening
      at
          the
             centre

I hear
no story
of their suffering
no rhythm
of waters running
blue St. Lawrence
breathing tides
the earth-red
of my own river
blending to
seed of lakes
the world
may wait
a hundred suns
to see

When my body
swings like a
dead tongue
from the white-man's
scaffolding,
will there be
an eloquence
to tell…

or will this
prairie be
a coffin
for my voice
a dwelling place
for

        two

          white

            stones?

## 5   The Last Word

Do our voices
reach out
from the past
escape the text
of history book
or turn
of politician's tongue,
describe a
true syllable
of what we knew
and still know
though words
are water
one can feel
and not define?

Or could there be
some secret part
of north
some centre
we never touched
in all our wandering,
some syllable
of silence
our tongues
did not dare
to desecrate,
some holy core
whose seed
we could not hope
to recognize as
            altars running
            fountains thru
            the deep
            earth-colour
            of our blood.

# Death at Quebec

*(The seigneur tells it)*

At first
the sun burned
our pink skin

warmth and
brandy-laughter in
the long house
Good Cheer, they said

our prayers
scented the
green chapel-wood

in there
I could smell
God

    with *him*
    our muskets make
    the silence jump back
    (it grows again
    seamless   self-healing)
    striding thru drifts to
    the brown doe
    dead against a
    hump of snow
    back-broken, like a stick
    oh the blood-sweet
    dark venison of her
    our beards drip
    with it
    *his* mouth: a wound

Every year a child
grows out of her
like a tuber

a corn-blight sucking
nine months on the
stalk of her, but
ruptured spores breed:
the wind diseased –
the stem of her green once
once cradling my lust
I rooted in her
summered on her thighs
she caught the rain of
my sperm   O God the
ground gave way and we
both survived

Last night…again
she took it in her clay
crotch (like a carrot)
even my lust couldn't heal

    her prayers
    in the evening
    are sweet breathing
    are incense falling:
    my ears speak

These sons of mine
(I saw them red-skinned
birth-blood still on them
pink worms
crawled out of that
clay seam   only her
screams gave my ear
pain, made it all
at least animal)
where will they find
an image of knowing?

I see them now
on rivers of noise
on the Ottawa
on the Richelieu
brains worn smooth
with endless paddling
their souls gone
to the beaver
(or some darker furring
among the bronzed
grease-glistening whores
spread-eagled on every
hump of granite)

And my fat daughters...
leeches that
feed on my love till
the bone gleams
pain   shines

This land will
not breed corn
but flies thrive
drink the cool
sun in

I have one son,
he tills the
brutal soil
fumbles prayers on
his thick tongue
obeys me with his body,
tills the ground lustily:
but there is no marriage
of sun and earth here,
he cannot beat the fields
into submission
his rage withers the corn

        clay is stubborn
        loves pain

"Pray to God," his mother said,

But he too has looked for Him
behind the shadow
under the ice
in the blind sun

There he is now!
He's broken the share
snapped it cross-grain
fingers too calloused
to feel the seam,
his tongue moves easy
in a furrow of curses

I will tell him!

But these dreams:

        red-skinned squaw
        on the domed snow
        weakening where
        thighs cross
        articulate
        O God   the gun
        slides
            blood-wet
        into the sweet
        dark deer-meat
                of her...

Are these woods a
shadow around me or
in me?
the sun is thin with
shining thru them

This granite is older
than our first bone
is seamed with myth
with hieroglyphic runings
sealed by a silence
that stilled the
first and vital Word
(conspiracy of
sun   earth
and condoning sea)

This earth
made its covenant
with universal darkness
long before the God of
Abraham broke Chaos
with his lance
of light

Year by year
I sit
in the sun's thinning
my age growing around
me, the shadow
lengthens, grows
no darker, no
more light is let
thru the trees,
the dreams persist
but do not be-
come a dream,
will not give me
life nor death,
I watch my son
abuse the earth
he sprang from,
see his mother
stiffen because the
yearly child
no longer oils her

seam with blood,
think of my sons
dying graveless
the wind praying
over their bones –
somewhere a savage whore
tuberous bellied
full of black
spore the earth
will spit back at her
will spit back at me

because I sit
year by year
watch the seasons
rot and revive

The sun is
keen today
against the leather
of my skin,
is clean

and casts
no shadow

out or in

# Brebeuf on the Cross

This pain
scrapes me
clean
(bone-knife skimming
pulpy flesh
from the hide:
oiled gleam is
holy in the sun)
makes life single
and singular:
>  blood   guts   bone
>  fuse on its point
>  merge with its
>  purpose   the
>  purple altars are
>  running with pus the
>  steeples burn
>  thru bloody cloud

This pain is
bearable and believable
delicious as
Eve's first and
only apple
my teeth squeeze
the white flesh
surrenders the
bitter and teeming
tumescent heart
at the core

my arms
break like
rotten crosses

*My Christ,*

do You hear them?

* * *

Was my Saviour's death
so absurd as this?

I dangle from
this crooked stake
like a scarecrow
without the authority
of even clothes –
the crows drop
their dung on me
with divine disdain,
savage laughter
rings with the
terrible innocence
of the child seeing,
I want to
giggle at my
own nakedness:
     withered testes
     strung like unpicked
     grapes on a vine the
     sun never loved,
     not even the wind
     could frighten my penis
     into standing

My crow children
come unto me
with gifts of pain
that are
invisible strings:
I dance to
their mad puppetry

At last
my mouth gathers
all of its godly rage,
I utter one cry
just as the vine
discovers its
lost tumescence

even the jack-
pines blush.

Is God peeking?
does He feel
these strings
jerk childishly
in the face of
my ludicrous agony?

* * *

When the flowering stops
will the roots
be fingers
grounded in firmament,
or are they
of this exquisite burning
this delicious blood-blossom
which consumes
               me

I feel it
carolling in my
private darkness
             harmonic
             and
             pandemonial

O God!
is this grand
death Yours or
my own?

# La Salle: Fragments from a Journal

## Part One

In March of 1680, LaSalle along
with four Frenchmen and an Indian
hunter set out on a thousand mile
journey from Fort Crevecoeur on
the Illinois River to Fort Frontenac
on Lake Ontario.


Out there
it seems so peaceful:
hot sun and icy lake
blend
without complaint,
trees release their
hoarded light

out there
the bush gathers
darkness, death
is numerous and
without sound:
      no word to mark the
      end of things
      and no one
      listening…

but

beneath this conspiring serenity
what scenes of
pantomimic terror?
what acts of wordless fury?

They do not know
the wood has already
devoured them
beaks have picked out
eyes for berries,
claws tasted flesh,
cold nested in
the marrow-warmth

heat has brooded
too long in the
cellulose chambers,
lightning flooded the
cranial rooms:
cells are not
       waterproof

They do not know
melon-seed is
spilled semen the
ground spits back

winged   burred wind and
water-blown seed
salts flesh,
uproots capillaries
broods an embryonic
dream of death

(pine-cone is a
wire worm in the
flaccid penis:

crows make it
their carrion home)

They do not know
wind sings insanity
to the listening brain
the sun is a
bright leech the
heart loves

and winter dines
on the warmth
a bone leaves

* * *

I've seen the
slick of my blood
on dead rock:
berry-juice for
lewd tongues,
wandering bear (or sun)
to lick

We don't feel truth
till our gut breaks
of it
and we die
with the stink
in our mouths

* * *

Tonight
I ordered them
not to light it

they think that I
and not the cold
am their enemy

But snow's pain
is impersonal:
I can feel
the shape of my
bones where the
flesh was,
they are
              comfortable

After a while
we despise

        fire

        * * *

Cold, like pain,
is a companion
he puts the blade
in lovingly

leaves the
bone clean

        * * *

They are drowsy,
want to sleep:

it is their death
wishing its way
into the brain

Cold gives me
the clarity of pain,
when I walk
I know an outline
of bone
angle and direction
beneath the
superfluous flesh
become believable

* * *

Sun and snow
have made light useless,
the brain pulls
its eyes inward
to warm and
illuminating darkness.

When it is time
I will let
my body sleep:
the mind knows
where it is going

* * *

What is blizzard
more than inner
curves moving,

a darkness
in reverse?

* * *

Tonti:
your iron claw
cuts two ways

inner wounding
like a foreign scar
you must continually
enclose with your
nativeness,

and

outward first
by which we all
know you,

Even I
must shake that
rigid claw, feel
the flesh that
closes it

        * * *


Pain gives a
form, is a
kind of knowing,
a direction we can
only contain
or occasionally
      oppose.

My will
is my wound
outer and inner:
　　　granite and distance
　　　the unloving total
　　　quality of this land
　　　is apocalyptic pain
　　　my body
　　　　　contains

　　　* * *

Moving
is its own space
my pain fulfills

and love is
a kind of
moving

　　　* * *

This wind is a
blizzard of blood
a harvest of nails

I
　love them

　　　* * *

This stretch of
rock and evergreen
these endlessly
stationary rivers
are distance
are time

are the real cross
Christ stretched his
body on

And his Agony
is our going together
thru a winter garden
with its stations of
ice and snow
(sun abandoned,
wind rehearsing doom
in the pines)
is our mutual blood
left against the
centuries of trees,
is repetition of our
scarred feet on
millennial granite,
is the shared energy of
our walking
which is become
a voyage
(not to water-
falling innocence,
a Great River's source,
not to the hewn
and blocked sanctuary
of European pride)
but a voyage
which is no longer
a voyage at all
but a
journeying

## Part Two

In 1684, LaSalle, with four ships
and two hundred colonists, attem-
pted to land at the mouth of the
Mississippi River. However, they
missed their target, and landed
in Texas. Several attempts were
made to find the River, and on
the last of these LaSalle was
murdered by a group of conspir-
ators from his own party...

This south-
ness winds into my flesh
rains in my blood
builds a private storm
each cell magnifies
each nerve articulates

the brain cannot
contain...

Ah, Christ,
where is your
northern and sheer
bone-directing
love?

        * * *

Remembering that other journey...

river spurting and
strong like a
cut artery

they grumbled
more than usual

strange that I
never feel the
strain of muscle
the tortured palms,
except when we stop
and the pain comes
in great ejaculations!

Do I keep it
locked and sacred
in some inner space
to be spilled, later,
on the ground?

On the water
there is never pain,
at least, not mine.
Perhaps I share
the river's

Each tree brings
its own face:
I see their
angular pain,
their bevelled and
elongated pride,

the wind in
them is incessant
ancestral whispering:
I feel their
cranial longing:
tribal nerves quiver
in my glacial dark

sudden flood of
sun   ice
articulates at last
bones of the
dead centuries
move in these
faces move in
me

The river below us
flings its brown arms
over the shouldering granite:

here, all land
is island,
water encompasses and defines
the current that
carries us so
wilfully is
line and direction

I put my paddle
in and feel the
tilt of the sea.

How can I tell them
we can be lost —

do not know what
island of rock
will be brought
eventually to us —
and yet be
found because the
river is both
brine and blood
and ocean is
ultimately human?

\* \* \*

They think we are
lost again...
and we are

but the river
has a mind
of its own

\* \* \*

They are crazed with it,
dragging that
Indian doe
into the green bush
jamming their
European tubers into the
nest of her groin...

She sheds them
like disused leaves and
the bush welcomes
her greeness back:
a wound received.

They lie there now
in a semen daze:
limp dreams in their hands
do not tell
the implacable vengeance
of granite and wood.

Inside
my own seed
boils in
scrotal darkness
drives its pro-
genitive longings
back thru blood:
they sear my
brain like
hot stars like
cosmic
branding irons.

\* \* \*

They are plotting again,
who will put the
first bullet in my brain,
who will give me
an insignificant end.

They do not know
the magnitude of
death.

* * *

Here, death is
palpable —

a slit throat
blood still bubbling
white bone
shining thru the
cruciform core

or the carcass
of a stag
gutted by wolves
(did he believe
his death even as
the Roman jaws
embraced his throat,
loved his blood?)
or that Senecan chief
and his family
found in the
northern spring with
snow's release:
gathered still
in a last
supper of pain
a kind of
communal dying
(did they,

having tasted enough of
hunger   winter,
at last
love death?)
eyes still open:
to let
the universe
in?

* * *

One is lost
not when the place
is strange,
only when direction
fails

* * *

They are whispering again:
I am arrogant, they say,
they plot against me,
hope to humiliate me
with the King.

They cannot know
*my* humiliation:

I am naked
on the stake
of the universe,
shiver in
polar winds,
continental elements

conspire against me
the sun is sprung loose
from God's orbit,
the land and I
are Armageddon
without end,
together we tear off
lids from the Seven Seals,
apocalyptic horses
thunder inside us

we hurl our
separate cries back thru
Chaos and the
dying Light
to the first
presumptuous atom

a cry that is
our arrogance
our selves loosed
from tides-pull
from the systolic screams
of sun and blood

surely this is
Christ's cry flung out
at the centuries
from a pair of
crossed sticks stuck
in a mound of dust

while the cosmic
thunder laughs

surely this
is the ultimate
arrogance

\* \* \*

My death is
south
insinuating
sheer bone

and moss
on the north side
of my brain.

## Saying Grace: An Elegy

*For my mother*
*Grace McWatters:1917-1972*

## 1

At my birth
we shared the
same pain

your blood
rubbed my eyes
open to light
heaved in
the dark
rushed out with my
my cry as your

scream squeezed
the lights shut

       * * *

When I burst
headlong into this
world my
lungs exploded
just as your

appendix burst
like a time-bomb
ticking in its
womb

only one of us
made it whole.

\* \* \*

Thereafter
for the longest while
you were my village
the paths to the gravel
to the lawn's end
were only as long as
your arms could reach,
shadows from the trees
were the cool spray
of your hair against the sun,
wind tangled
in the dark hedges
was a terrible anger
compressed in your words,

but mostly it was love
leading us both and together
down to the lake's edge,
to look out and over and
never see the other side,
feeling (as one) the waves
tremble at our feet

like small cries
smothered in their own sound,
and their terror went through me
deliciously liquid
(safe I your hand
till I felt it
tremble)

I can't remember
who let go
but the rending came
like a small
       smothered
            cry

We turned

My village was complete


## 2


That day
when I touched your dead hand
my skin quickened,
out of habit I whispered
in your ear not wanting
to wake you too sudden,
but you lay there
        aloof
dissembling sleep
insisting even when I
shook your wrist
like a stick (refusing breath:
no man / husband / son
would waken you that day)

after a while
it occurred to me
you were not there:
the casket of your flesh
confirmed it.

But when I turned
to the window, to the
morning behind me,
you whispered, "Don'tworry."

         \* \* \*

Presence / absence
are equally unreal

in the half-dream
before sleep your
voice, your face,
words we both
understand, and when
the room comes back,
the half-light
but enough
I call after you,
want to tell you
wait, there is

                more. . .

         \* \* \*

Presence is
more than flesh
warm or cold
and absence is
more than loss
or the sum of
grief, the love
not yet told

\* \* \*

I bear them both,
believe nothing

# 3

If money is king
you showed them
you died with
nothing

not even dignity

\* \* \*

Death does not
"take us", it
moves welcome
into waiting spaces

\* \* \*

My dreams lie:
bring me your smile
in a casket

\* \* \*

Guilt is death's
bright shadow

I can't look
at the sun

**4**

The Greeks they say
dreamed grief:

coined it on that
perilous stage
ode and palinode
thru the thundering mask

histrionic / hysterics
loud enough just
for the gods who
caused it

At times, alone
I want to bellow
like Hamlet the Dane,
let the world know
whose anguish this is and
what cause, what cause . . .

Quiet corners
in the room
receive my cries

give them back
like applause

gods have always had
the last laugh

* * *

Feeding grief:

I lie awake nights
inducing dreams:
scenes from the past
when you were still my mother,
we laugh till the camera
clicks off:

swimming at the beach or
picnics in Canatara or
riding together on
tilt-a-whirls, our
screams merge and it's
all in jest
(but laughter is
one-sided; would these
scenes be crossing
your last dream
whose good times
did you remember?)

So, I summon
happy scenes only,
stoking my grief:
I must know ho
deep it goes,
how much is
        mine,

and if I find out
I want you
to look first

    * * *

The tragic scenes
come easy,
bring no relief
just guilt: not
because I was
there or wasn't.

(we are all complicit
with death)

We watched you
dying day by day,
as you watched us
though your eye gave
nothing away and
we were too polite
to speak out of turn

Then who should say first?
Give it a name?

Who now bears the guilt
For that silence?

*this* silence?
                my shame?


## 5

Girl / woman / mother
no sign of what
must have been there,
what was to come,

I make this album
instead of poems

Photographs tell
such easy lies

One photograph
I shall keep for myself:
the girl on our porch
with fresh-cut flowers
and a smile too bright
for the camera's simple eye

But what if this one?
your father, the grandfather
I never saw (though he
saw me, you said)
Len McWatters: posed
beside the cannon in our park
(the War of 1812? The Fenian raids?)
so grand and proud,
his Irish twinkle so
life-like he could step
right out onto
Christina Street,
his strut unimpaired
by sixty years on a
yellowing photograph,
and I would run up to him,
fling my six-year-old arms
around him and introduce myself,
and we would stroll back to the Park
and have our picture taken
beside a friendly cannon

What else do you do
with an old photograph?
Of a grandfather you
can't remember meeting?

And you, who remembered
the man, the cannon, the picture,
you who died and
left us both unremembered,
what are we to do with you?

It's okay for him
father and grandfather:
he can stay locked
and yellowing in an
old photograph, his
smile looking out
over sixty years and back
(who knows?) to the Fenians or further,
smiling until the last
McWatters has died,
smiling until the paper
cracks it

How lucky for him
to say your name
from morning till
morning: singing it,

a tongue made
human with
                    naming

But what do I
alive and remembering
                    do?

              * * *


Just once
I'd like to
say grace and
believe it


# 6


Pain writes poems
on a human face,
crooked lines,
scrawled flesh.

We make poems
with our skin / our bones,
words obey
dance the tune
of our pain

How many lines
must I scrawl
from the mask
of your runed face?

And what grace
in obedient words,
transfigured pain?
What gain
when we both die
in the rending syllable
of the last poem?


# 7

In my backyard
tulips heave the
surrendering ground,
gin air

Inside each leaf
a coiled green syllable, the
rendering bud.

Further back
in the drowsy orchard
children climb
the apple-trees,
fill them with their
loose-limbed anonymous
laughter.

In the distant grass
cockrobin opens his

beak like a cup:
drinks his song.

Beneath the garden /
lawn / orchard grass
earthworm cleans the
earth with its body,
its lean appendix.

Further down
further nameless seeds
cleave, seek the
orphanage of a
new world.

In the west
the sun goes down
unflinching,
a blown blossom:

and I toss these poems
fresh-cut
on my mother's grave.

**Don Gutteridge** was born in Sarnia and raised in the nearby village of Point Edward. He taught High School English for seven years, later becoming a Professor in the Faculty of Education at Western University, where he is now Professor Emeritus. He is the author of more than seventy books: poetry, fiction and scholarly works in pedagogical theory and practice. He has published twenty-two novels, including the twelve-volume Marc Edwards mystery series, and forty books of poetry, one of which, Coppermine, was short-listed for the 1973 Governor-General's Award. In 1970 he won the UWO President's Medal for the best periodical poem of that year, "Death at Quebec."
Don lives in London, Ontario.

To listen to interviews with the author, go to: http://thereandthen.podbean.com.

Visit his website at dongutteridgewriter.com.

Email address: dongutteridge37@gmail.com.